THE DR. HIGGINS GUIDE TO HEALTH & WELLNESS

THE DR. HIGGINS GUIDE TO HEALTH & WELLNESS

PHYSICAL, EMOTIONAL, INTELLECTUAL, SPIRITUAL

Dr Evelyn Higgins

ISBN: 1503290506
ISBN 13: 9781503290501

TABLE OF CONTENTS

CHAPTER 1

DOCTOR HEAL THYSELF

HEALTH IS MORE than simply the absence of disease. Please re-read that line. Bold but true. We are not healthy one day and sick the next. Rather, how we live each day can boost our health or inch us toward disease. I'll even go as far as saying we don't have a health care crisis but rather a crisis in how we think about health care. We, in the good ol' US of A, consume half of the world's pharmaceuticals, yet we populate roughly only five percent of the planet, according to the documentary film "Doctored."

Considering those numbers, you might logically think otherwise. If Americans had stellar health, I'd say why change what works? But we don't. We rank 47th in life expectancy according the *Central Intelligence Agency Fact Book.* So what's the disconnect? Why is a first-rate country like America listed so low on the life-expectancy list?

Albert Einstein reportedly said, "The definition of insanity is doing the same thing over and over again expecting a different result." I'd say Einstein would call us crazy. We don't yet have the numbers to prove what we are doing works – but it's evident that a portion of the health industry wears myopic blinders.

What's lacking is *prevention.* Unhealthy lifestyle choices lead to illness and/or disease and the "solution" is a pill or surgery.

Now for my disclaimer. I will never advise anyone, "Absolutely no surgery or pharmaceuticals." The fact is, both save lives. The problem is abuse rather than proper use. In the wellness model we teach exactly that: wellness. I can't say it enough - the key ingredient is a dose of prevention.

NON-STOP PROPAGANDA

Let's consider what goes on day in and day out in America.

Pharmaceutical companies spend a fortune marketing drugs to physicians and the public. According to estimates from a Johns Hopkins Bloomberg School of Public Health study conducted in 2010, Big Pharma spends $27.7 billion marketing to physicians in America. In addition, as the industry's daily monitoring service Fierce Pharma points out, direct-to-consumer advertising racks up another $4 billion in costs (source: The Motley Fool, www.Fool.com). With that sort of advertising slapping the consumer in the face daily, it's no wonder the public believes the answer to good health lies in the magic pill.

According to the Center for Disease Control in Atlanta, 48.7 percent of the population uses at least one prescription drug monthly; 21.7 percent use three or more. Of the total number of physician office visits, 75.1 percent result with a patient leaving with a prescription. Also revealed in the CDC's study were the most frequently prescribed meds: analgesics (pain relievers), anti-hyperlipidimic agents (high cholesterol) and anti-depressants. In fact, according to the American Society of Interventional Pain Physicians, Americans consume 80 percent of the world's pain medications.

When I read these numbers, the questions raised include: Is our pain physical, emotional, intellectual or spiritual? Are these pains a side effect of other medications we consume or is it our cultural lifestyle?

As an alternative medicine doctor for 28 years, specifically trained as a chiropractor as well as a radio show host, I get a close-up view every day of the insanity. The more time I've spent on the airwaves, the more I've become impassioned to having a voice of change. Our one-size-fits-all method of healthcare is not in alignment with what I believe is realistic and human. The globe is home to seven-billion people, each with his or her unique DNA. Maybe, just maybe, we need to take a different track.

A QUESTION OF BALANCE

We need more than physical health. We depend upon emotional, intellectual and spiritual health as well. Hence, I've developed the Four Pillars of Health. Each and every component has a bearing on the other and must be in balance. The medical industry must view each person as an individual, not a symptom. The symptom may help us get to the root of the problem, assuming we are fortunate to live long enough to find it.

I was alerted to these Four Pillars when I myself became a patient. I experienced excruciating "symptoms" repeatedly within a 10 day period. I landed in the emergency room at the hospital and was diagnosed with a T.I.A. (Transient Ischemic Attack), commonly called a "mini-stroke."

Like many single mothers, I was no stranger to stress and mine had become chronic. According to the Merriam-Webster dictionary, the definition of "chronic" is "marked by long duration, by frequent recurrence over a long time, and often by slowly progressing seriousness." I can only see that now in retrospect.

My typical day: before I'd head to my office in the morning, I'd drive my daughter to school through Atlanta rush hour traffic, taking over two hours to go 30 miles. Inevitably, I'd be late for my patients. Working through the day until early afternoon, I'd do the reverse trek, knowing there was a good chance I'd meet up with traffic again and return to my office late for my afternoon patients as well. I arranged for someone to drive my daughter from my office to her daily swim practice while I'd continue to see patients until 7:00 pm or later. I'd then pick her up from practice, make dinner and after my daughter went to bed, I'd do my paperwork. My average night sleep was two to three hours. Until my body shut down.

First I lost my vision. I was eating lunch across the street from my office when interrupted by a shooting pain in my head that was no ordinary headache. For one hour I tried to muster the strength and vision to drive, but could not. I got across the street literally by the grace of God, telling myself, "If I can just get to my office and lie down on a treatment table…"

Which is what I did until it was time to see patients again. But in meeting with my first patient, I knew I wouldn't make it. Inside my office, I slumped at my desk, trying to get the pain to stop so I could continue to be the doctor and not turn into the patient. My attempt at "I'm stronger than this" was failing. My office manager came in and said, "Doc, you look terrible!" I slurred, "I feel terrible."

She called her husband, an EMT, who quickly diagnosed me, "You're having a stroke."

I knew he was right having watched this happen to my aunt. We drove straight to the E.R. and less than 20 minutes later, I couldn't walk or speak. After a series of tests, the original diagnosis was confirmed: I had had a T.I.A.

And while my speech returned as did my ability to walk – my eyes were opened like never before. The attending doctor got my full attention when he said, "There's a good chance you will have another one within 10 days and possibly a full blown stroke – but this time you won't recover." At 46 years old and a single parent, I surrendered. I became my own doctor. I was one of the lucky stroke victims. "Doctor heal thyself" became my mantra. Of course, there was the emotional and financial stress, but you get the picture.

THE PATIENT IS ME

I began to study and learn all I could about T.I.A.'s. After tremendous research to learn about the neurotransmitters and how the brain chemicals work, I attended a medical seminar and used my lab work as subject for my study. When reviewing the data with the head scientist at the lab – remember, I wanted to learn -- he asked, "Is the patient on any meds? These values are very extreme."

"No," I said, "and the patient is me!"

To which the scientist went silent. I need to point out that these labs were taken at a time when I had already taken three and a half weeks off work to rest. I was feeling good enough to return to work. But obviously, I was not actually good enough.

It was time to study even more and learn how to realign myself into what would become my Four Pillars of Health.

Today, whenever I give talks on this episode of my life, I show my lab results on the screen and say, "I have the patient's permission to show these values." By the time I reveal the patient's identity, silence overcomes the room.

"On the outside I look healthy," I say in response to the wide-open mouths staring at me. My cortisol levels (stress indicator) flat-lined to the equivalent of a person who never gets out of bed, never mind-functions on the driven level that became my normal life.

But really, it was a life turned inside out – and the start of my personal passion for the Four Pillars of Health. This was also a first-hand view of what our healthcare system can and cannot do. First off, my experience shows me that the so-called "healthcare system" is adequate at crisis care, acute care, diagnoses, triage, hospitalization and pharmaceutical management for life. But it doesn't focus on *health* itself.

Health truly is more than the absence of disease.

CHAPTER 2

PILLAR ONE: PHYSICAL HEALTH

LET'S START WITH physical health - the easiest element to change among the Four Pillars of Health. It may take work, but the route is laid out. It's also the one pillar that Western medicine has thoroughly studied, as evidence by the data and diagnostic tests available to doctors.

Given current medical data, I ask you to consider this question: Do we consume the pill or does the pill consume us? Should the fourth leading cause of death in America be fatal drug reactions from prescription drugs in our evolved society? Should the leading cause of death be a disease that is actually preventable through old-fashioned efforts like exercise and eating well?

As you already know, my idea of health has an all-encompassing perspective. I prefer to use the entire arsenal of what makes us humans healthy. If after we try all conservative means to achieve health and for some reason still don't achieve it, then by all means I go with the Western approach. But first, we must exhaust the conservative options, ones that utilize a functional approach, a grass roots base, if you will.

They help focus the guesswork in a fully studied health picture. You know exactly where you stand and that alone should be disseminated to the public. Just as valuable is the research offered by CAM, the California-based, research institute which focuses on complementary and alternative medicine, and reports that drug companies spend $57.5 billion on marketing pharmaceuticals to the public. That, they also report, is actually double what is spent on research and development (R&D). In addition, nearly $61,000 is budgeted for promotion targeting individual physicians. It's clear that the industry is focused solely on solving health concerns with prescriptions rather than prescribing lifestyle changes.

These tests that I will describe later tell us about what obstacles or imbalances are in our body. Just as I described earlier, no two people have the same DNA, it is also true that no two have exact test results. So, doesn't it make sense that no two people should have the same exact treatment as well? That is a very different approach than our current culture suggests today, prior to reading a book such as this. Given the different starting points for each individual, a tailored lifestyle and diet should follow. Working with a doctor who actually takes the time to access your Four Pillars may seem idealistic - but he and she does exist. That is how I treat patients.

Your health is your most valuable asset. Don't settle. Without it, even a wealthy person realizes there is only so much one can buy. All the money in the world cannot fix an unhealthy heart or set of lungs. Prioritize health. No excuses!

We will expand on lifestyle diseases, including the obesity epidemic, as we discuss what each of the four pillars represent. The first step is to have a paradigm shift in our logic. For example, we don't have a headache due to lack of Tylenol; we don't have depression due to lack of Elavil; we don't have osteoarthritis due to lack of Celebrex; we don't have ADHD due to lack of Ritalin. I think you are getting the picture - we have such symptoms due to real deficiency balances in the body.

CHAPTER 3

PILLAR TWO: EMOTIONAL HEALTH

TAKING CARE OF your physical body is the first step towards a strong foundation for emotional health. The more we learn, the more we realize the body-mind connection. The stronger the body, the healthier the mind. The opposite is also true; as the spirit withers, so does the body. Just as exercise improves the heart and lungs, it also improves your emotional health. When the brain is oxygenated through exercise, it thinks clearer. The mood is also lifted through exercise by powerful chemicals called endorphins which biochemically and physiologically alter your emotional state. The point: you have the key within yourself to unlock these chemicals. The world's best drugstore resides within you. There is no co-pay, no deductible and you don't need a prescription. Just like the game show - The Price Is Right!

My goal is for everyone to easily access this information and realize that we face a severe problem. According to the Center for Disease Control, by 2020, the second leading cause of medical disability will be depression. As of writing this book in 2015, nothing is being done differently to address this epidemic other than everyone waiting until 2020 when I'll say, "Told you so." Again, Einstein wouldn't be impressed.

Depression is now considered the "common cold" of psychopathology. Seven out of 10 adults report stress and anxiety. Sixty-eight percent report a sleeping problem. Three-fourths of females with stress report physical problems such as headache, gastrointestinal upset such as Irritable Bowel Syndrome, shaking and hot flashes, unrelated to menopause symptoms.

When we prescribe 254 million prescriptions at a cost of $10 billion on antidepressant medications according to the CDC, second in volume only to cholesterol lowering drugs, and know the problem is multiplying by the day - it's time to make a change. Currently, conventional psychiatry diagnoses a patient based on what the patient or their family reports and or the doctor's observation. There is no objective testing.

The point: this method of prescribing medication is no better than a stab in the dark. How many times have you heard the professional say, "We'll try this…"

My prescription: we should not *try*, we should *do* – especially if we have the objective data tests at our disposal. If anything, what's revealed is the result of an often apathetic and/or financially-driven system of medicine. Furthermore, when the solution is still not achieved – even after prescribing a maximum dose of drugs (when the symptoms become intolerable), this form of medicine seems counterintuitive.

When patients who suffer with fatigue symptoms (while using western medicine) come to my office, it's my goal to determine the health of their adrenal glands. I test for hormone deficiencies and look at the observable data on specific neurotransmitters, (brain chemicals such as dopamine and serotonin, for example). I would use neuromodulation to effect specific brain chemicals, while the patient experiences no side effects from pharmaceuticals.

Each neurotransmitter has a specific function to make the brain work properly – a prerequisite to allowing the rest of the body to work optimally.

Given the rise of ADD (Attention Deficit Disorder) and ADHD (Attention Deficit Hyperactive Disorder) as well as other brain imbalances like anxiety and depression, we expect these problems to multiply. What we are currently doing is ineffective. Diagnostics tests are available to measure the various neurotransmitters and then show a trained physician where the imbalance lies. It's inappropriate to take a "stab in the dark."

Popular treatment in today's culture for the ADD and ADHD patient consists of -- what else -- psychotropic medications. The diagnosis would come from a description by the parent of the child or the patient him- or herself. ADD and ADHD pharmaceuticals are created to effect a change on specific neurotransmitter imbalances, (that is, NT's such as dopamine, serotonin, and epinephrine), yet we don't know which one(s) we are trying to modulate because we have not done the objective testing. The primary "test" is the observation of the parent, teacher, or patient themselves describing in their words their experience. What if the parent or teacher has a different scope of vocabulary than the student? This would create a different picture of what the student is experiencing, with perhaps a different course of treatment. What if there is more than one imbalance? How about when the side effects of such pharmaceuticals are suicide? Parents, teachers and students all need to know what tests are available. There is more than one way to treat a problem.

CHAPTER 4

PILLAR THREE: INTELLECTUAL HEALTH

PEOPLE TYPICALLY THINK of intellectual health as academic knowledge alone. It is, in fact, so much more than a trivia contest or an SAT score. Intellectual health involves creativity, critical thinking, problem solving, general knowledge/education, as well as common sense. Last but not least is the skill of adapting to change.

Often the person with the greatest intellectual health succeeds just as far or farther as the person with high grades simply because of the demands he or she faced in life. Life experience can enhance intelligence, creating the sweet spots and balances that lead us to fulfilling and healthy lives.

Everyone has heard about history's most gifted people – those who performed poorly in traditional academic testing, let alone never achieved valedictorian upon graduation from high school. Think Albert Einstein, Abraham Lincoln, Richard Branson, and on and on. Somehow our culture continues to label students with low IQ's and/or SAT's as "unintelligent."

Hence, the subsets of intellectual health I mention above. Just as your IQ can come from your DNA, so does your instinct. It is wired in your cells. People such as Babe Ruth or Derek Jeter in baseball have it right off the bat - with no pun intended. That's instinct and raw talent. Your cells are designed with instinct. That's why our bodies know how to work. Many researchers define instinct as genetically hard-wired, not learned or conditioned.

INTELLIGENCE AND INSTINCT

Two of the most memorable moments illustrating this intelligence instinct was during a brilliant full moon in Jupiter, Florida. I watched a mother turtle come out of the vast Atlantic Ocean to lay her eggs past the shoreline. Seeing this giant, prehistoric majestic creature crawling through the sand to find the perfect spot to lay her young was a living breathing moment of instinctual intelligence. Months later, I watched the eggs hatch beneath the brilliance of a full moon and witnessed the tiny turtles make their way into the vast ocean to start their new life. This was nothing short of awe inspiring. If you've never witnessed it, I suggest you put it on your bucket list. It is a display of instinct at its finest. Beautiful. Natural. Simple. The survival instinct we all possess. It is the strongest instinct we own. Think how humans are hard wired for food, water, and shelter, for example.

The difference between intelligence and instinct is that intelligence can explain it but instinct can find it. Imagine how powerful our society would be if we could marry both? I can offer you intelligence, but not instinct. And it's my opinion, you can heighten your intelligence by fine-tuning and working your Four Pillars of Health. It's synonymous with the saying "leaders are born, not made." I believe the greatest of the greats are born. I also realize we have large service academies like the Air Force Academy and West Point that try to mold leaders with much of that same mentality. It's the reason these institutions exist.

Now we get to wisdom, which is both intelligence combined with instinct and a totally different level of that smarts. Bishop T.D. Jakes said, "Instinct is the treasure map of the soul." I couldn't agree more. When I heard him say that, I recognized the perfect visual: instinct is what leads us to opportunity; wisdom is knowing what to do with it. Just as the physical pillar can blend into the emotional pillar, so the intellectual pillar blends into the spiritual one.

CHAPTER 5

PILLAR FOUR: SPIRITUAL HEALTH

THE SOUL IS the softest intellect of all, but also the most powerful. At heart, it's what drives us. I believe we live in a lost society on many levels, but that we can change this if given direction - just as with your physical health. Listeners and patients tell me over and over again in different ways that our priorities are so off kilter.

Historically, the age group most disgruntled in life are seniors, complaining how the golden years were anything but golden. Equally paralyzed are Baby Boomers who report mid-life crisis and their own loss of magic. Their stories are similar: life is no longer the gift it was designed to be; it just happens. More and more, those of us in the health field hear teenagers and children also describe a creeping and paralyzing sensation while asking, "Is this all there is?" and "Isn't there something more to life?"

My belief: each age group has bought into a false set of values – driven by the accumulation of possessions, titles, honors, awards and money. These, they believe, are the cultural treasures guaranteed to deliver happiness.

The truth is that old cliché: it's in the journey. It's about *how* we gather those possessions that matters.

TEACHING CHILDREN HOW TO DEAL WITH LIFE

Here's a personal story illustrating these societal norms today. My daughter was invited to a college recruitment session at Georgia Tech, an academically superior school specializing in engineering and looking to attract more females. At the break-out session for parents, the recruiters informed us of their findings: "Your daughters all have the grades and intelligence to survive in this competitive atmosphere. What they need is the ability to think for themselves." The recruiters blamed the sheltered lifestyles that many of those students lived which intercepted their ability to find and test-drive their natural talents and intelligence for themselves. They were talking about digging within for true instincts and abilities.

A parent asked the recruiter, "Can you tell that to my daughter?" After a momentary laughter from the audience, the presenter responded, "No. That's your job."

How do kids discover their own spine when parents do all the heavy lifting and cater to their every need – buy them their first car, pay their apartment rents, (need I go on)? How do kids today discover any sort of pride or fulfillment when their first job pays nearly that of their parent?

Given our society's design for immediate gratification as well as the fast-tracking possessions – thanks to parents buying their kids into the "right" college, the "right" friends, and so on - the most important feature is missing. The joy and sometimes pain of "getting there" by accessing one's own wits. That's a personal journey.

It's in that journey that kids identify the feelings of pride and satisfaction, as well as the experiences and meaning behind the five senses. That's being alive.

THE DOOR TO THE SOUL

The soul is what connects us to our own unique human selves. We are able to interact and feel, to experience and to imagine much more than our five senses could ever offer.

It is the ability to relate, compare and contrast the perspective of that which we see and feel which is where the door to the soul opens. Soulful people tend to be magnetic. They can feel fulfillment with other human beings as they feel the vibration of joy in themselves, as well as others. Their energy field is bigger than who they are. These are people with a presence. It is not an exact definition. It is within the realm of poetry, myth and suggestion.

The soul says I am me, with features all my own. It is the part of you which is most intimately you. Even more than your emotions. The soul is the underlying source of all motion you create. Motion is life. This explains why the soul prefers hints rather than declarations, because it truly is the master of possibilities. It has its own compass. Souls can make something that logically appears like it would never mesh and somehow weave it together. It's creative and divine. Its shear principal is multi-faceted. Even when the soul is orchestrating changes, it is paradoxically the haven for safety. So now, think of when you are not sure of something and feel like everything is contradicting. That is your soul speaking.

The ability to appreciate is the first step to realizing profound value. It is the dimension missed by most. The soul is the prism through which we look deeply into something and discover its value and deep underlying purpose. And that purpose is uplifting to yourself and often to others as well. The soul is the force that tells us to touch hearts and make the world a better place. That is why our composition has been given a soul. It's survival for mankind. The soul is the seat of wonder.

THE WONDER OF IT ALL

So often people minimize wonder. In fact, so often people misuse wonder. They say "I wonder why he parked the car that way over there," when what they mean to say is "I don't understand why he parked the car over there." No wonder the magic has been lost. The state of wonder is awe. When we wonder we are not looking for answers; we are simply amazed. Think of wonderful, playful moments of beauty and fun. Wonder is the soul finding the eternal in a moment in time.

I end every radio show saying, "Your heart is the greatest healer of your life – and your soul, that's the heart of your life. Let's start living, folks. Today starts now." In that statement I'm saying the heart is both a physical as well as an emotional organ, and your soul is the epicenter of your life. That truly combines all Four Pillars – and it's my goal to teach you, personally, how I do that.

I believe we will one day look back at this time in history and realize that the current state of medicine is barbaric. Present-day, traditional medicine treats a disease, not a person. This current society needs help living healthily. It is my goal to teach you, personally, how I do that.

Change starts with desire. I promise you – if you have desire, I will offer the motivation, inspiration and education for you. Once you realize the value in each of the Four Pillars, your understanding will grow exponentially. You, and only you, can take the first step. And that first step is in action.

CHAPTER 6

PHYSICAL HEALTH PILLAR, ACTION STEPS

SEVENTY TO 85 percent of diseases are directly linked to lifestyle – heart disease, diabetes, osteoarthritis, and obesity, for example. That should tip you off to how you, and everyone around you, can have more control over health than currently realized. The simple truth is that we have all "life-styled" ourselves into disease – and the only solution to that is to lifestyle our way back.

That statistic mentioned above tells us that we are not looking at the causes of what ails us. If we were, then we'd see the link and hopefully aim toward prevention. Eureka - prevention!

"BUT... YOU DON'T UNDERSTAND!"

When I present this idea, this is usually where a patient defends his or her lifestyle, telling me that I just don't understand. "My mom, dad, brother, sister," (or actually, insert any relative here) with "xyz"-disease was "unfortunately born with this as their destiny." Then the patient tells me, "What you're saying may be true of others, but you don't know my circumstances."

What I've come to learn in my three decades of working intimately with patients is their link to relatives... specifically, the people with whom they live and interact with similar, often identical, bad habits. They often all share the same poor health. The sooner we realize that the solution is not with a magic pill but rather a change of lifestyle, the better we will be.

EPIGENETICS

Enter a fascinating area of medical science called epigenetics, the branch of biology that can influence a person's DNA, as well as that of their descendants. In reality only 10 to 33 percent of your genes play a role in your overall health. This is an extremely powerful insight into your physical self: you can alter the remaining portion of your DNA. Science teaches us that the non-genetic factors have great impact in how the genes express themselves. In other words, you have more control than you think. Take for example, a hypothetical piece of news that your fictional parents finally divulge: you have a predisposition to a certain disease.

It is at this moment that you would likely want to know the rest of the story: how to avoid the fate of this illness or influence its growth. I'm here to report that you are more in charge of your body than you think.

Epigenetics has taught us that. We can up-regulate or down-regulate our DNA, depending on the positive or negative lifestyle in our environment. (And remember - *who's* in charge of your body?)

In addition, new technology called genome testing allows scientists to redesign the strands of DNA so to enhance specific traits. For example, that has helped scientists identify the gene for alcoholism, or certain cancers. Combine this knowledge with epigenetics and we have opportunity to take a more educated path. It's for you to take.

Let's say you have a predisposition for lung cancer. That information is only of value to you if you make prudent decisions not to smoke, or participate in any other unhealthy behavior that would negatively affect your lungs. So, it all still comes down to you deciding to lifestyle your way to health. That is a lot to swallow, but once you start thinking your way through your day with this awareness, then you are taking the first step. You will up-regulate your DNA, designing a healthier self with this physical, emotional, intellectual or spiritual decision. You will take the first giant step toward becoming the healthiest version of yourself.

Let's take a close look at some of the more commonly diagnosed diseases today – chances are that any one of them are affecting a family member. Let's zero in on cardiovascular and or liver disease, cancer, autoimmune diseases, insomnia, depression, asthma, diabetes and arthritis. The one that kills more Americans than any other? Cardiovascular disease. And here's what "kills" me: it's both chronic and preventable. Yes, preventable.

Right now you should be asking, "How can a disease that is preventable kill more than any other?" By now, you should also know the answer: It is in the lifestyle.

We claim to be an evolved society, however our habits suggest we are not as intelligent as we believe. According to the Prevent Cancer Foundation, only five percent of cancers are hereditary. That means that non-inherited causes of cancer – that is, lifestyle choices, foods, and physical activity -- have a direct impact on our overall cancer risk. The American Cancer Society reports that half of all Americans will develop cancer in their lifetimes. The rise in autoimmune diseases has hit like a tsunami, yet we put on our blinders and allow them to run ramped and ignored. Patients exist with ongoing symptoms - life-altering bouts of exhaustion, mysterious incapacitating weaknesses, severe skin rashes... I could go on. And treatment varies from being labeled as a hypochondriac to a myriad of medications that never cure the problem. According to *The Autoimmune Epidemic: Bodies Gone Haywire in a World Out of Balance,* (Touchstone, 2009), there are over 100 autoimmune diseases at a financial burden of more than $120 billion, compared to the yearly health care burden of $70 million from direct medical costs for cancer. The research states that autoimmune diseases shorten the average lifespan by 15 years, referring to it generally as a western disease.

THE "WILD WEST"

"A western disease?" Now why is that? That is the question people should be asking, rather than "When's the fairy showing up to make it all better?" Many of the autoimmune diseases my patients and radio show listeners have addressed over the years were ones treated with traditional medicine. My observation? The solution is more an insult to the body – never tackling the root of the issue.

Take one of my more common observations – diet-related harm. I have witnessed more injured GI systems than I can count and feel strongly that they're mainly a result of poor diet. Our guts are exhausted. They have been used and abused. In short they are all washed up. They no longer have the capacity to digest without literally having a leaky gut from the vast amounts of toxins on every level of the Four Pillars of Health. The body is by design a self-repairing system but only if we give it proper care. And that requires a healthy diet. It's time to rid our refrigerators of toxins.

Interestingly enough, all of the lifestyle diseases have something in common other than being categorized as lifestyle diseases. They share inflammation as a precursor to the disease. This reminds me of a particular patient who I'll name Jane for the purposes of telling this story. Her lab work indicated considerable inflammation in her body. Her father, she had explained to me earlier, had died from both cardiovascular disease and cancer. When it came time for the consultation portion of our appointment, she asked, "Doc, what do I need to do to change this potential time bomb inside me? I want to live."

It was music to my ears. She was a walking-talking example of what brings me to writing this book and working long hours. She understood that the solution was up to her to implement into her lifestyle. We immediately designed a plan of lab work, specific exercises and eating guidelines. And today – some six years later – I can tell you that her tests show measureable improvement.

It is my belief that our injured, irritated guts are the window to many diseases. And our choice to heal or exacerbate that is in our hands (or really, our mouths).

SLEEP DEPRIVATION

Eight out of 10 Americans claim they suffer or have suffered from insomnia. When you consider American's poor food choices, lack of exercise, and technology-driven frenetic society - it's little wonder. Those of us in the medical field are always consulting lab profiles with either brain chemicals or hormonal imbalances, or both. The fact that we have tests to uncover where these imbalances lie and are not utilizing them is nothing short of criminal. When you discover that sleep deprivation has been used in warfare history as a form of torture so to coerce a prisoner of war into informing captors of certain truths, then that notion should awaken you (no pun intended) to the power of sleep. With the current lab work available to doctors, we can correct the imbalances with neuromodulation. Patients report how their sleep is restored, literally allowing their cells to heal overnight and their electrical system to recharge.

TYPE 2 DIABETES

Let's talk about Type 2 diabetes. Here's a disease which impacts roughly 30-million people at a cost of $245 billion a year – and, may I add, in the past five years there was a 41 percent increase in the population. Sadly this is a lifestyle disease Americans can easily prevent through a healthy diet and an active lifestyle. You don't have to be a scientist to see that this disease is "being fed" around you. Just go to a fast-food restaurant or a county fair and stand in line for a meal.

The answer is available in our homes and shopping carts. But what's lacking is the action of change. The research – both sociological and scientific -- is pointing us all to this necessary starting point. But without action, it's meaningless.

Sure we offer medications – and at an epidemic level. But the emphasis should be on coaching people. Reversal is possible because the majority of Type 2 diabetes is due to the obesity epidemic. According to the CDC, 69 percent of the adult population is overweight. Frightening. Equally as frightening is the obesity trend in the pediatric and adolescent population. This is spinning out of control. And I fear the solutions are spinning away.

We are currently witnessing the first generation of children who will not outlive their parents. That is shameful. Healthy food is integral to good health. When you think that two-thirds of the world is dying from too much food and one-third is dying from lack of food, it's obvious what this planet's priority should be.

Both asthma and arthritis are in large part related to the obesity epidemic as well. All of these lifestyle diseases are linked to the way we live our lives. I mention this *not* to point fingers at individuals, but to inspire the notion that good health is available if you make healthy choices.

TOXINS

Toxins are inevitable in our lives, but we need to limit our exposure to them. Unfortunately, we are exposed to them on an ongoing basis. Environmental factors are a major contributor to lifestyle diseases like cancer, diabetes heart attacks and more. Degenerative diseases such as Parkinson's and Alzheimer's are linked to toxic free radicals in our body, which damages our DNA structure. Of course emotional stress is another toxin-creating source in our bodies. Depressive or angry emotions fire up our body to release chemical reactions that can weaken our neurological, hormonal and immune function. A prime example of this is when cortisol levels rise with stress and eventually create an imbalance leaving the body without enough resources to function properly.

When the medical community discusses toxins, patients sometimes feel overwhelmed and out of control with the vast amount of information. Do not fear. Everything we ingest or absorb into our body – toxic or not -- must be eliminated. As I stated earlier, the body is designed to be a self-repairing system, even if our bodies are chronically assaulted. And the assault can spring from everywhere - from toothpaste, shampoo, lotion and antibiotics, PCB (polychlorinated biphenyl), radioactive compounds, to pesticides laced in dairy and other foods. Even our thinking. One thing's for sure: there is no shortage of toxins in the world.

When we don't allow our bodies to heal naturally through healthy, non-prescription choices, it should not be surprising that we experience slow, creeping dysfunction leading to disease. Perhaps by now, you are beginning to see how everything is connected and how the body is designed to work in balance and harmony... if only we get out of our own way.

We are living in an age of contradiction. We use words to describe the importance of health, we ensue national battle to get it right, yet we don't share the info the taxpayer has worked for to better ourselves and truly place the individual at the epicenter, rather than the almighty dollar.

When I travelled to India, I saw so many examples of a nation of contradiction. Despite an ever-present reverence for the sacred life of a cow, women and children slept in the streets, stacked one by one. And this I witnessed as I was whisked through the streets in the dark of night by rickshaw on my way to an opulent hotel. Once I arrived at my destination, I was asked to walk through metal detectors then searched by military guards carrying machine guns.

Back in the United States, I'm troubled by a different set of contradictions: "early-onset adult issues" invading the minds and bodies of our young population – some inspired by our celebrity-driven culture. What is the message we send a 16-year-old when she asks for – and receives -- a set of breast implants for her birthday? Is this the parents' attempt to give a gift of self-esteem, or is it the teenager's self-esteem (or lack thereof) run amuck? What does this say about the health – both mental and physical -- of a nation? Is this the way to ring in the 17th year of life -- or is this a red flag signaling concern? All the while a different kind of epidemic is growing – that is, more and more youngsters suffering from diseases usually associated with the older generation – diseases such as cancer, diabetes, and even cardiovascular disease. One day, as I was prepping for a radio show on heart disease I was seeing stats of children on Lipitor that were truly insane. That was when I asked myself, "Why isn't anyone shouting STOP?"

ACCELERATED PHYSICAL AGING

Accelerated physical aging is not natural. It is the result of our chronically ill society suffering from degenerative diseases. The good news is we can repair it, if we get out of our own way. The science is available to measure the damage.

Biomarkers such as the shortening of the telomere length – that is, the tip of the chromosome that's often compared to the shoelace which keeps it from fraying -- tell us how we are aging. Popular tests exist which measure the elasticity of our arteries. The most-simple aging test is measuring hormone levels. The good news – this can be done at home. We don't lack the diagnostics, we lack the educational follow through.

Dr. Raymond Francis, a noted MIT chemist, author, health advocate and guest on my show, goes as far to say that the increase of Alzheimer's disease is 90 percent related to anti-depressant drugs. In other words, an assault by Prozac. Is this to say that no one should take Prozac? No. It's to say that everyone who consumes pharmeucticals for emotional and mental well-being should consider alternative measures. One issue with anti-depressants such as Prozac is that people continue on such medication for infinite periods of time. That is, in part, where the damage begins. We don't use the meds as they were designed. If used at all, they should be short term with a program of strategies that teach the patient to realign their lifestyle and Pillars of Health.

CHAPTER 7

ARE VITAMINS AND SUPPLEMENTS REALLY NECESSARY?

"You can trace every ailment, every sickness, and every disease to a vitamin and mineral deficiency."

— Dr. Linus Pauling, two-time Nobel Prize winner

Dr. Mark Hyman, whose best-selling books and PBS specials have ushered him into an expert position in the medical and health fields, often speaks on the optimization of food's nutritional value. In *10 Day Detox Diet*, (Little, Brown and Company, 2014), he suggests, "If people eat wild, fresh, organic, local, non-genetically modified food grown in virgin mineral-rich soils that has not been transported across vast distances and stored for months before being eaten...and work and live outside, breathe only fresh unpolluted air, drink only pure, clean water, sleep nine hours a night, move their bodies every day and are free from chronic stressors and exposure to environmental toxins, then perhaps, they might not need supplements."

I'm afraid that's a fictional life. I know of no one, including myself, who lives the perfect lifestyle in the perfect environment.

DRUMMING UP CONTROVERSY

When the nightly news lacks a crisis-of-the-week, like clockwork, it hauls out the vitamin controversy story. Typically, a dramatic storyline suggests that vitamins and supplements have no nutritional value, despite the fact that half the adult population takes supplements and vitamins. Nearly always left out in the reporting of the story is the integrity of the supplements and the sources of the raw material. Are they chemically made or derived from a natural plant base? And if they are chemically made, then what are we actually ingesting? That, in my opinion, is at the heart of the story. The real story. However, the chatter some news organizations stir up is clearly directed to make headlines and raise headlines at the cost of valuable information.

Equally as important in this overall discussion is the integrity of the source for the story. Everyone knows that certain magazines at the grocery store checkout line are not necessarily interested in your health – but rather in selling copies of their publication. Their headlines may target the lack of a mineral in your diet, for example, on why you are feeling fatigue. Or the story may be written in such a way that you are convinced if one capsule of a vitamin is good, and that two must be better.

VITAMIN DEFICIENCY

Every vitamin and every mineral creates a biochemical reaction in the body. Many vitamins utilize co-factors to successfully create the desired outcome in the body. For example, let's consider the great job the press has done in educating the public about vitamin D deficiency. The fact is that 85 percent of adults are vitamin D deficient. That's a story that was heavily covered across the various media outlets. As an aside, the latest research tells us that obesity can lead to a vitamin D deficiency. Given the stats I provided earlier that sure does make sense. This is how the snowball rolls into the snowman.

The conditions associated with a vitamin D deficiency include adrenal insufficiency, Alzheimer's and Parkinson's, allergies, autoimmune diseases, cancers including colon, breast, skin, prostrate and 14 others, depression, diabetes, heart disease and hypertension and the list goes on and on. I use the vitamin D example because it is such an easy fix. Vitamin D is inexpensive and readily available as a supplement. Equally as important is supplementing with D3, specifically cholecalciferol, rather than D. The reason? It breaks down into calcitrol, an important cancer-fighting supplement.

Overall, vitamin deficiencies are typically easy fixes and cost-efficient. According to Vitamin Angels, a non-profit organization that combats malnutrition around the world, an estimated 190-million children under age five globally suffer from vitamin A deficiency, a major underlying cause of child mortality. Furthermore, it costs just 25-cents to reach a child with vitamin A deficiency for one year and will increase his or her chances of survival by 24 percent. According to Howard Schiffer, founder and president of Vitamin Angels, the general public believes that vitamins exist to optimize health rather than actually make a difference in life and death.

Natural ingredients are obviously the way to go; adding more chemicals to your body is counterproductive to healthier living. These examples below illustrate my point – despite what you may read on the label:

- **The synthetic source of vitamin A** - made from methanol, benzene and petroleum esters.
- **Vitamin A from a natural source** - made from fish oils, carrots, lemon grass and spinach.

    What would you prefer? Personally, I'd opt for the orange carrot as opposed to methanol.

- **Synthetic vitamin B6** - may contain petroleum ester, along with hydrochloric acid and formaldehyde.

    Personally, if someone offered me a dose of formaldehyde, I'd wonder just how much they liked me.

- **Synthetic vitamin B12** – get this: may contain cyanide. Yes, cyanide!
- If you asked me would I rather have my daily dose of cyanide, or rice bran, brewers' yeast, liver or molasses, I'd happily go for the rice bran. You get the idea.

Now, obviously we are talking about small amounts of cyanide for example in these supplements – too small to kill you. However, why ingest any? It doesn't make sense, especially, when we have other ways to get the benefit of the vitamin.

CHAPTER 8

THE ROLE OF GMO – GENETICALLY MODIFIED FOOD

GMO FOODS HAVE become grounds for great debate. So-called experts argue these GMOs were created for the starving nations of the world. The problem? We still have starving nations in the world. In fact, they are increasing in part because of greater income disparities.

I believe if you become educated in this area, then the decision is simple: do you want GMO foods or not?

GMO uses a very dangerous herbicide - the most dangerous of all, glycophosphate. This product cannot be washed off as it becomes integrated into the plants' cells. From the plant, it integrates into your body. And that's how easily food becomes a toxin.

Conversely, food can also be powerful - just think Super Foods. (For a list of Super Foods, see page 41.)

DIET FOODS AND BEVERAGES

Have you ever noticed that the typical person ordering a diet soda is overweight? Research on this subject suggests that diet drinks disrupt the body's ability to count calories. The sweet taste increases the body's hunger.

As Hippocrates said thousands of years ago, "Let thy food be thy medicine and thy medicine be thy food." Nothing could be closer to the truth.

Let's look at the obesity epidemic. Two-thirds of adults are overweight or obese. Studies have revealed that certain diseases are directly related to obesity. So you can conclude that healthy foods in appropriate portions can contribute to healthy living. For many consumers in the United States, the knife and fork are the tools of mass destruction.

CALORIES

The answer to weight loss, is this simple and time-tested. If you want to lose weight, cut back on calories.

If it takes 3500 calories to add a pound to your frame, then reduce your calories. If we reduce our diet by 500 calories per day (or exercise away 500 calories per day) we'll safely lose one pound per week.

When my patients journal their food intake, they see clearly how their choices affect them. Journaling, an effective tool for anyone wanting to lose weight, allows you to see in black and white what foods to eliminate. All you have to do is make the change. And commit to changing.

SUPER FOODS

Try to add a few of the Super Foods to your diet daily – a minimum of five or six servings of fruits and vegetables. While I'd rather you opt for nine to 10 servings a day, I accept that change is hard and the best approach is one step at a time. We are each at a different starting place. However, everyone must begin somewhere. So begin. Below are suggested Super Foods and the sorts of fuel they literally bring to your table and body.

Apples: contain slow acting sugars, which keep you feeling full longer.

Blueberries: rich in healthy compounds and said to help prevent obesity. Research suggests blueberries act as an anti-aging food.

Carrots: naturally sweet, easily used for snacks, sides or additions to soups.

Eggplant: a great source of fiber to help digestion.

Figs: lower cholesterol; a great source of calcium.

Grapes: lower high blood pressure and cholesterol.

Squash: helps strengthen the immune system; adds a glow to skin.

Kiwis: compared to the orange, a kiwi is even richer in vitamin C. It's virtually fat-free.

Leeks: rich in folate, antioxidants and a good source of B6, vitamin K and vitamin C.

Melons: contains an enzyme believed to reduce stress. (Bring on the cantaloupe!)

Nectarines: provides your daily requirement of vitamin C.

Onions: immune boosters, even just one or two a week.

Peppers: contain three times the power of citrus fruits when it comes to vitamin C. (Side note: try eating a yellow or orange pepper like an apple - they are surprisingly sweet.)

Quince (the fruit that looks like a pear-apple combo): known for its anti-allergenic and anti-inflammatory properties.

Red raspberries: contain a good amount of potassium, iron and magnesium.

Strawberries: loaded with Vitamin C.

Tomatoes: loaded with lycopene (the chemical that gives fruits and veggies their red color) and a cancer fighting food (cancer of the prostate, breast, lung bladder, colon, and pancreas, for example); also credited with preventing heart disease, hardening of the arteries.

Watercress: a good source of B vitamins which helps with mental functions.

Disharmony occurs when you and your body are in a state of lacking - whether lacking acceptance, joy, and/or balance, for example. Disharmony is acute when it occurs in the present moment. It becomes chronic when it infiltrates you for an ongoing period and on every level of your life. The key to prevention of this on a chronic level is awareness. Become an observer of your day-to-day physical, emotional, intellectual and spiritual health and habits.

Food is no different. Become aware of your habits – and that starts with awareness of thoughts and actions. To do so, keep a journal. The road map becomes visible as we begin to lose unnecessary weight - and then benefit from the rippling effects (such as a lighter mood and physical ease).

Food is the most abused anxiety drug. When you have a hankering for a specific food, this is a physiological yearning based in part on the balance or imbalance of the chemicals in your body. The hormones, the neurotransmitters (such as dopamine, serotonin, and epinephrine, for example), as well as other elements of your body help your brain to make its choice. The goal: reach a balance. If for example your serotonin is low (usually resulting in a low mood), you may reach for an orange for example. Without realizing it - unless you start to live in an aware state - you reach for a serotonin-increasing comfort food which will help you feel better. Food becomes the medicine. This is where the understanding of the Four Pillars becomes paramount.

Just as I stated earlier, food is the most abused anxiety drug. Exercise is the most underrated anti-depressant. This brings us to the role of exercise in our daily life.

CHAPTER 9

OUR BODIES ARE DESIGNED TO MOVE

LOSING MUSCLE IS a normal part of aging.

Once you accept this, it's easier to literally take the first step toward slowing down this natural state of growing older. Therefore, if you realize this, that is really accept it, then you can take the action to slow it down.

Muscle mass begins to degenerate at roughly one percent per year after age 25. Even the performance of elite athletes declines greatly after age 40. By 80, approximately 50 percent of muscle is lost. *Fifty percent.* Knowing this should inspire you to ask, "What do I need to do to intercept the inevitable?" And we're not just talking about this from a vanity standpoint, but rather the ability to maintain one's physical frame (and by the way, independence) with aging. How many times have you heard about a senior person suffering a fall? So often, medical professionals connect that to an elder person's weakening bones. Unfortunately, they also often observe a quality of life spiraling downward after such an incident.

Strength Training (ST) is key to combatting brittle bones as we age – and especially lifestyle-friendly for those who say they don't have time. Allow me to make it perfectly clear: this is *necessary*, not just suggested. Even if you must wake-up 20 minutes earlier in the morning – and, in the very least, on your calendar three times a week. If you are lucky and find a workout that you really enjoy, it'll be easier to make this your new way of life.

Delete the vision of Arnold or Popeye with bulging muscles. That does not happen to everyone. Such musculature is based on genetics and diet. We can, however, all get stronger and prevent the kind of injuries that can take us out as we age.

I am such a strong proponent of Strength Training (ST) because of research that indicates ST has been found to have a beneficial impact on gene expression - not only slowing aging but actually returning gene expression to youthful levels in seniors who start resistance training.

Strength Training is no longer just to look and feel better, but to reap the benefits of slow aging. According to the *Beginners Guide to Strength Training*, "ST is an integral part of any well rounded exercise program regardless of your age and gender." It has additional benefits – from losing excess fat to maintaining healthy bones and preventing muscle loss as we age.

And it also changes your molecular, enzymatic, hormonal and chemical levels of your body. It has systematically helped to slow down - and even reverse - diabetes caused by sedentary lifestyles. Sadly, if I were to write about the medication that's commonly prescribed to reverse diabetes, we would all want stock in the company. The numbers of patients who take it is staggering.

I know with full certainty that even a disease such as diabetes can be reversed with proper Strength Training. And that is why I bang my drum louder. Strength Training also helps Alzheimer's, osteopenia and cardiovascular disease, our greatest killer.

According to exercise experts Dr. Doug McGuff and Phil Campbell, those with cardiovascular disease should not shy away from strength-training. In order to benefit the cardiovascular system, you have to perform mechanical work with your muscles.

Research in recent years suggests that aerobic exercise -- swimming, walking and even running, for example -- is one of the least effective forms of exercise. For those who are time-strapped, take note: these are usually the most time-consuming activities and may even be counter-productive. High Interval Intensity Training (HIIT) has risen to the top as the most effective exercise. HIIT integrates with Strength Training to maximize cardiovascular benefit.

Unlike when catching a plane or a train, you're never too late to start an exercise program. The earlier you do this in your life and with consistency, the greater the long-term rewards. And look at it this way: by extending your lifetime, you'll have more time to exercise.

Note to Mom and Dad: lead by example. It's the best gift to give your children. An active lifestyle reaps rewards year after year.

One study showed Strength Training in the elderly reversed oxidative stress and revised 179 genes to their youthful levels. It genetically turned back the clock 10 years. Guys, this is huge. Please utilize this information and don't just read it. As Gandhi said, "Be the change you wish to see in the world." An added benefit: you're guaranteed to eat and sleep better once you put ST into action.

Strength Training not only builds muscle strength and elasticity, but also strong connective tissues, tendons and ligaments. From an aging perspective the proper muscle tone which results from Strength Training allows for greater biomechanical improvement in your muscles and connective tissue to hold your body in position, which will lessen injuries and falls.

Another huge benefit of Strength Training is that the body burns calories – and get this: up to 72 hours after you exercised. Not only that, it creates profound effects on insulin and leptin sensitivity, HGH (aka, the Human Growth Hormone, or also commonly described as the "fitness" hormone). This alone should be a reason to get moving in the area of Strength Training.

CHAPTER 10

EMOTIONAL HEALTH,
ACTION STEPS

As I SAID earlier, the physical pillar is easiest to tackle. The emotional pillar becomes more challenging. Physical health has widely accepted tools for self-improvement without making the individual feel vulnerable or those around them uncomfortable. The emotional pillar is different. While we Americans are slowly improving our ease with addressing emotional health, we still consider it taboo to discuss psychoanalysis and twelve-step programs. In the very least, the dialogue has been started.

Your emotional health is synergistic with your physical health. Just as all Four Pillars are complimentary, physical and emotional are also. They are entwined like the age-old question "Which came first - the chicken or the egg?"

Think back to what you learned in the Physical Pillar Action chapter. The increase of hormones and brain chemicals you drum up with physical exercise will directly affect your emotional health. Your DNA can be up-regulated... and that will improve your health. It's a balance here. I'm vigilant about our physiology being balanced before emotional health can be optimized. A balanced physiology is the building block for emotional health.

PARADIGM SHIFT

Let's take a look at two buzzwords associated with brain chemicals in today's culture: serotonin and dopamine. Either ring a bell? These are only two pieces of a larger neurotransmitter pie. So it is equally as dangerous to think the answer to every emotional imbalance is caused by these two and these two neurotransmitters only. Truth is - they *all* play a role in your health.

The reality of today's health care paradigm needs a shift. Here is a typical patient scenario: he or she visits the doctor with symptoms of depression; no zest for life. Through no fault of the over-worked doc, the patient gets a three-minute consultation after the physical exam and walks out the door with a mood elevator. You know how the thinking goes: "Let's pick one, quickly, so the paper-work can get done," and then the doc can move on to the next patient. Next patient comes in and says, "Doc, I just can't get off the couch. I don't love life." Same prescription, next patient. Without having the proper objective tests done, although available, the doctor is shooting a cannon at the patient hoping for the best.

Modern technology should eliminate the majority of guess-work and hope from science. Yet, this is not how we practice. Because no two people have the same DNA, that is, neither share the same lab profile, yet we treat them the same way. Are you starting to see the picture? The doctors have good intentions, but the system has expectations that, to be met, a patient need to be in and out in five minutes. Of course, this doesn't include the waiting!

As a system, we are great at treating emergencies and utilizing high-tech, life-saving techniques. We are not good at wellness, plain and simple.

The following is a list of the neurotransmitters that most commonly run through our brains and a quick description of how they affect us day to day.

CLINICAL CORRELATION OF NEUROTRANSMITTERS

Glycine, like GABA, helps calm and relax the body.
High levels:
• Anxiousness • Low mood • Stress-related disorders
Low levels:
• No associated clinical symptoms to date

Epinephrine, also known as adrenaline, is important for motivation, energy, and mental focus.
High levels:
• Sleep difficulties • Anxiousness • Attention issues
Low levels:
• Fatigue • Lack of focus • Difficult weight loss

Taurine is important for heart function, healthy sleep, and promoting calmness.

High levels:

• Hyperactivity • Anxiousness • Sleep difficulties

Low levels:

• Severe hyperactivity • Severe anxiousness • Severe sleep difficulties

Norepinephrine, also known as noradrenaline, enhances mental focus and emotional stability.

High levels:

• Anxiousness • Stress • Hyperactivity • High blood pressure

Low levels:

• Lack of energy • Lack of focus • Lack of motivation • Low mood

GABA, the primary inhibitory neurotransmitter in the brain, is necessary to achieve calm.

High levels:

• Hyperactivity • Anxiousness • Sleep difficulties

Low levels:

• Severe hyperactivity • Severe anxiousness • Severe sleep difficulties

Dopamine is responsible for pleasure and satisfaction, as well as muscle control and function.

High levels:

• Poor intestinal function • Developmental delay • Attention issues

Low levels:
• Addictions • Cravings

Glutamate is the body's primary excitatory neurotransmitter, necessary for learning and memory.
High levels:
• Anxiousness • Low mood • Seizures • An immune response
Low levels:
• Fatigue • Poor brain activity

DOPAC is a critical metabolite of dopamine.
High levels:
• Hyperactivity • Focus issues • Stress • Developmental delay
Low levels:
• No associated clinical symptoms to date

Phenyl Ethyl Alanine-PEA is important for focus and concentration.
High levels:
• Mind racing • Sleep difficulties • Anxiousness
Low levels:
• Difficulty concentrating • Difficulty thinking clearly • Low mood

Serotonin plays important roles in the resolution of mood, sleep, and appetite.
High levels:

• SSRI medications • Stress
Low levels:
• Low mood • Sleep difficulties • Uncontrolled appetite
• Headaches • Hot flashes

Histamine helps control the sleep-wake cycle as well as energy and motivation.
High levels:
• Allergic responses • Sleep difficulties
Low levels:
• Fatigue

5-HIAA (5-Hydroxyindoleacetic acid) is the primary metabolite of serotonin involving monoamine oxidase A (MAO-A) and aldehyde dehydrogenase, an enzyme.
High levels:
• Intestinal complaints
Low levels:
Impulsivity • Sleep difficulties • Low mood • Cravings
• Urges

NO EXCUSES

Once we have the patient's lab work evaluated, reality offers the proper lens. This is not always an easy report for patients to hear. The truth is - we all have a story as well as an excuse for our thinking and our actions. Here's the simple truth: if your goal is be healthier, then you just need to listen and learn from it.

Let's pause a moment to think this through.

It is my belief that most of life is within our control. The problems happen when we somehow give our power away. That's not always on purpose, but the end result is the same. By simply changing our thoughts in a more proactive and positive way – and baby steps at first -- we can realistically change our emotional thoughts for the better.

The average person has 60,000 thoughts a day. Of those, 85 percent repeat over and over. If these are negative and repeating again and again, imagine what you are training your thoughts to believe? It's as bad as those obnoxious television commercials you see over and over.

Now, take a deep breath and read, and then reread, this next statement: the most influential person you talk to all day is yourself. Yes, yourself.

You are the only one that can actually re-tool your self-talk and change it to be positive and proactive. If you are making negative statements about yourself, all day, every day, then what do you imagine the outcome to be? How many times a day do you tell yourself, "That was dumb…" or "How stupid are you?" or "I really should have…."?

Stop for a moment and ask yourself if you spoke to your best friend that way, would he or she remain your best friend? For most of us, the answer is no. So why should you settle for anything less? Improving the way you self-talk is the first step toward emotional health and a habit that needs to change today.

Awareness is the first step. New thinking is the next. (And don't be surprised if you take one step backwards after two steps forward. Such is the process of changing a habit.) The sooner you begin, the sooner you'll enjoy the effects. The results are tremendous and the cost is free. The ROI (return on investment) would make Bill Gates and Warren Buffet want in!

TOXIC PEOPLE

Next - the effect of toxins on your emotional health. And we are not just discussing chemicals. We must consider people, that is, *toxic people*. When you lack the tools to build walls between you and a toxic person, you allow them to physiologically alter your body's chemicals. Take time to inventory family, friends, work associates, and any others who offer you a negative vibe. Think hard about who needs to exit your orbit. Yes, it's time for spring cleaning - even if it's not spring.

Not always easy, right? I know that is true. And this is where you must rely on your instincts as well as your smarts.

This is usually where most people defend the insanity circling their lives. They literally defend it with their life because of negative effects of emotional toxicity. Abuse - whether it's physical or emotional - has no place in your life. Toxic people charge in and ruin lives – their own as well as those around them. This is where you must ask yourself the difficult question, "Do I love myself enough to change this? Have I experienced enough pain to change? Isn't it time to put up a boundary with this toxic personality – and tell them 'Enough is enough'?"

Just like how our physical health often mirrors those with whom we spend free time, so goes our emotional health. Sure, genetics play a role, about a 10 to 33 percent influence. Just like physical health. But that remaining 67 to 90 percent is what *is* in your control. That larger portion is for you to create and put into your own head.

Most humans function with "mob mentality," that is, we take on the behavior of the people around us. So you see, the power to up-regulate or down-regulate your DNA has been in your control all along. You just need to become aware and choose the right path. It starts with you.

Only you can judge your situation and answer truthfully. There's no need to make a specific declaration to anyone, well, that is, anyone other than yourself. This is about you and your health. Of course limitations do exist. Take for example, the amount of control you might have with a bully, abusive, OCD boss. That sort of dynamic requires smart strategy – if you wish to keep your job.

Patients I consult know my mantra: "Don't make your life harder by creating more stress." Working with an insane boss can be stressful enough - but losing a job can stir up even more.

Remain in the situation and learn to reframe this person's words and behavior. When the boss opens his mouth, train yourself to hear the voice of Charlie Brown's teacher – that is, instead of words, tell yourself that what you hear is a muffled horn. This is "behavior modification," a cognitive technique that when learned properly, will help you build your resiliency. (If necessary, you may seek extra guidance from a coach, psychologist, psychiatrist, counselor, clergy or a best friend.) Remember – commit to loving yourself enough to make a call to action.

NEUROTRANSMITTERS

The neurotransmitters are the first step to measuring the physiological state of your emotional health. From there, we examine the need to change the habits and behaviors, realizing it can only be done one day at a time. Being cognizant of how you really think during your 24 hours is the awareness component. Realize what you allow into your mind actually affects your physiology. By taking control – with or without the help of a professional -- is like having the teacher guide you through a test. Your life becomes more manageable in every aspect every day.

Difficult people are difficult, no doubt. But look at it this way: when someone shows you who they are, believe them. Too often we humans try to change a person or a situation, even when it becomes an emotional drain. Let go. (That's your ego telling you that you can change them.) Don't give them credit for what *you* wish they were. Wait, watch, observe – and believe their actions. Simply believe.

A resounding truth for people is that we all want to matter. Even those who choose evil acts, do so to be recognized. One day, I believe we will have the ability to actually measure the hatred or kindness that comes from our words. Today, we can feel them and know the power they have. They flow from our mind to our being.

GOSSIP

Gossip is toxic. Think of the sort of scenario in which it's usually shared. The tone of conversation is usually a dramatic flair, or whisper. Gossips do it because they want to matter. They become important for knowing something someone else doesn't. They become a powerbroker. And it's a disease. A lifestyle disease. When tempted to gossip, remember that there are three kinds of people in the world: 1. Small people talk about people. 2. Average people talk about things. 3. Great people talk about ideas.

Be an idea person. It is a choice, just like the majority of choices you have when realigning the Four Pillars of Health. Your health.

"Be of this world, but not in it," is a phrase often cited by theologians – and often said by those far brighter than me. I just try to make a conscious daily effort to live it. Live with my fellow humans in the various communities

I enjoy – whether that's family, friends, office associates, or a volunteer activity.

Social media has changed the landscape of communication. Just like anything, there's good and bad. While it gives voice to the voiceless, it also easily allows people to engage in passive-aggressive and damaging behavior. Those who never had the strength to cut someone down in person can now take their grievance to social media. It's like the Wizard of Oz whose appearance on the big screen is frightening, but when you glimpse behind the curtain, you see that in reality, he's quite meek and putting on a show.

A tool I use often is journaling. Give Facebook a rest and journal. It's communication from you to you. Relish who you really are. And if your life story needs to be re-written, then write the vision of who you want to be and watch the pages come alive. We are each a best-seller. Choose to write a best-seller rather than the trash novel to be your life. Best-sellers live on. Trashy novels die.

CHAPTER 11

INTELLECTUAL HEALTH, ACTION STEPS

*"If you treat an individual as he is, he will
remain how he is. But if you treat him as if he
were what he ought to be, he will become what
he ought to be and could be"*

— JOHANN WOLFGANG VON GOETHE

JUST AS EMOTIONAL thoughts -- healthy or unhealthy -- affect your state of well-being, so does your environment. From the music you play, the literature you read or the art you view, they all have the same ability to up-regulate or down-regulate your DNA. Research proves that all of the arts have an effect on your physiology. Though it's nearly a completely virgin territory to most. Think about it: when was the last time you went to a museum, live concert, or reading at the library? How about the last time you took out CDs to study a new language or listen to a recorded book? All of the above can be free, so there's

61

no financial burden. (Of course you can also attend a class at a local college, though often at a cost.) The point is - get out and stimulate your brain. Create a better version of who you are at this moment.

Research tells us that art and music affect every cell in our body – and instantly. It changes the immune system and blood flow to all organs. Art and music can also realign your perception of the world, changing attitude, emotional state and pain perception. They create hope and "positivity," even help you cope with difficulties. They transform a person's outlook while changing the balance of the brain chemicals.

Another part of your intellectual health borders on the emotions. I discuss it here because of how your decision-making and daily habits can have rippling effects on the creation of your life. Your intellect and emotions seesaw together and directly influence your life.

To clear the cobwebs out of your emotions and fine tune your intellectual health, ask yourself at least these two questions about your behaviors: Which are reflective of your childhood? Are there any that it's time to consciously let go of today?

Certain behaviors are detrimental to your life, but have become normal. Even negative energy can feel normal. Despite your overall energy, it steals from your well-being. It's time to recognize this for what it is.

Once you see the list of answers in front of you, think about how you may reframe these habits to bring fulfillment and happiness in your life?

This is an area where journaling helps. Whether goals, lifestyle choices, or habits, the more we articulate and see the words, the clearer the problems. First comes awareness, then comes the strategy for action.

As Albert Einstein said, "We cannot solve our problems with the same thinking we used when we created them." If this rings true for you, then it's time to rewrite your reality.

While some issues that linger into adulthood may have started as scarred emotions earlier in life, we now understand the pillar and its physiological relationship with your brain chemicals and hormones, as we take the first step and work on changing the biochemistry of your body. It's now time to do the cognitive work and change for the better. The more you work it, the greater your ability to better your life. Once the neuro-endo-immuno-logical aspects of your physiology are under control, the cognitive choices are usually healthier.

Gratitude is an example of one of these choices. Too often people ruminate over what's wrong in life rather than what's right. It's the old glass half full half empty theory. The danger with ruminating negativity is that we begin to hard wire these negative thoughts and events into our story and worse, waste time.

If you hate your job, or your life, it's time to make changes. This is where patients tell me, "Yes – but, my situation is different. I can't follow the job of my dreams because of 'xyz.'"

That "xyz" is not anything but your "teacher." Yes – teacher. It's demanding that you find the answers to creating the best life you can. Start with baby steps – whether it means going back to school, finding scholarship money, or deciding it's time to commit to a diet. Make a list of all the possible steps - the small and the large – so to better visualize the details necessary to bring you closer to your more fulfilling reality.

Successful people visualize their optimal lifestyle, the one of their dreams. Visualization takes time. And I believe it's the first step to helping the mind see a new you before taking the necessary actions. Once you begin this visualization, then you'll realize the body-mind-spirit connection through the PEIS pillars, that is Physical, Emotional, Intellectual and Spiritual. After that, it all becomes fun and play – a game where you live your dreams. Equally, dreaming and visualizing negative aspects of life may also make them real. It is important to be aware of what you put in to your thinking is what you'll get out of it. You've heard the phrase, garbage in, garbage out; it applies to thoughts as well as food sources.

CREATIVE VISUALIZATION

The starting point for creating a desired life is in your imagination. Think about how your day would begin. What time? Allow for the details to unfold. What about breakfast? Or meditation? List the tasks you wish to get done that day. Think about who would be included in your day personally as well as professionally. By dinner, what would you have accomplished? What activities would you leave time for? Before you went to bed, what would you do? If you're not living the life you dream, ask yourself what limits have you put on yourself for that to occur. Which old habits are unnecessary today? The more you write, the more you dream, the easier it is to visualize, and therefore the easier to see. The easier it is to see, the greater the chances of living the life of our dreams. When you take responsibility for what it is that holds you back, you'll recognize control. And once you see that, you can change. It's time to rewrite your story.

Now, perhaps it's obvious why I suggested the creative thinking and activities to improve your health. A creative brain finds healthy ways to improve health and well-being. You can chose violence on TV or in the theater, or you can choose positive uplifting stories of personal triumph which can be emulated in your own life. The choice is yours. Start to notice the choices in every pillar – and realize that they are available to make.

Here's how we know we spend way too much time on violence. The average child has viewed 8,000 murders on TV by the time he or she finishes elementary school. By the age of 18, the young person has seen a whopping 200,000 violent acts, according to research complied at California State University. I believe there is a relationship between real-life violence and the increase of violence on TV, the big screen, as well as computer games. In fact, that increase fosters desensitization. We certainly have already seen the effects on physiology by outside influences in preceding chapters. Without a healthy and concerned society for children, why are we surprised that they are in desperate need of direction and leadership?

If a child plays violent computer games, you can easily imagine how that impacts their personal life. Just turn on the nightly news and take in all the school violence. It's time we all wake up and stop the insanity.

THE RIGHT CHOICE

It is not easy or convenient to make the world healthier. It is, however, the right choice.

If you practice gratitude in life, regardless of your starting point, and live each moment working towards "positivity," then don't be surprised by the bonus joy and possibilities.

When considering your goals, think both intrinsic as well as extrinsic. Intrinsic is the deep, enduring relationships. Extrinsic goals are achieving fame or a superior reputation for something. According to University of Rochester's study entitled *The Path Taken: Consequences of Attaining Intrinsic and Extrinsic Aspirations in Post College Life,* intrinsic goals are associated with a happier life. Those with extrinsic goals -- without working on the intrinsic as well -- suffered more negative emotion, such as shame and fear. They even suffered more physical maladies. The moral of the story is it's always about balance.

Consider the famous bumper sticker that reads, "Shit happens." I know you've seen it. I also know you've experienced it. Sometimes life happens through no fault of your own. It's simply, well, life – over most of which we have control. A suggestion I've given patients as well as radio listeners is to rate their negative events on a scale of one to 10, with 10 being the worst possible scenario. Now reframe the event using the worst possible thing you imagined (also on a one through 10 scale) – and see what you learn. I find most of us lessen the number on the scale after review. This simple too can kick-start your new life. As long as you do it.

A great way to change a low "dashboard reading" is to think about how you are operating, that is, how you are feeling both physically and emotionally. Again, using the one through 10 scale, with 10 being the best. If you assess your day at a level five of joy, for example, stop. Ask yourself, how can I pump this up to a level six? Or go higher -- an eight, for example. Then ask yourself, what's holding you back from making it a nine?

If you are old enough to remember the 1979 movie "10" with Bo Derek and Dudley Moore, you know the storyline concerns a middle-aged man who is mesmerized by the sighting of this ideally beautiful woman. The concept of "a 10" exists in how we lead our lives. Truly, when living with joy, you bring it to others. Such is the trickle-down effect. And in becoming aware of this, here's the extra reward: you learn how to discover even more joy.

ACCEPTING REALITY

Living with awareness allows us to live in the now. And that is what brings me to my view of the number one mistake people make in their lives -- resisting reality. (Another way to put that: the unwillingness to accept.)

We all have a different reality. Learning to accept our circumstances -- rather than spending wasteful time resisting them (much of which we cannot change) -- creates greater emotional and intellectual health. This action will take tremendous honesty on your part – a kind of inventory where you ask yourself how you respond to adversity.

Research tells us that those who respond well to perceived adversity and adapt to the new circumstances of life live longer and healthier. Again, it comes back to choice. I'm not saying it's easy. I am saying it's up to you to discover this and learn how to implement it in your life.

Since we're talking numbers, let's discuss the five-minute rule. As kids, we all know the five second rule: if you dropped a piece of candy on the ground, you'd pick it up and chomp it down anyway, claiming that it was on the ground for only five seconds or less, and therefore safe to eat. Enter the five-minute rule: if something is truly negative, allow it to be negative. Let yourself experience it -- but only for five minutes.

At five minutes and one second, move on. Turn the adversity into advantage. By doing so you benefit yourself and others. If you stay in your negative experience and ruminate, you empower your negative story. Don't allow that.

Learning to accept what is, rather than wallow in what you cannot change, gives you the power. When you turn off a painful experience/feeling after a quick five minutes, you also feel control. You feel power. This is the paradox of acceptance. You can shift to joy, and then enthusiasm. This is how you intellectually change your behavior.

GRATITUDE

Another intellectual choice is living with gratitude. When you live a life with gratitude, you live with happiness. Day by day you begin to view life as a gift.

As I said earlier, I close every radio show by saying, "your heart is the greatest healer of your life, and your soul is the heart of your life. Let's start living, folks. Today starts now."

When you live with a positive synergy -- with passion, purpose, love and gratitude -- you create energy in your life. Allow yourself to live your amazing life. The potential is right there.

CHAPTER 12

SPIRITUAL PILLAR, ACTION STEPS

LASTLY, THE SPIRITUAL pillar, the most complex of all. Imagine that -- a doctor saying that this component of health is more complex than the physical. The spiritual pillar houses the complexities of you, the mysteries that make you YOU. Add to that all the potential that you can't even imagine yet!

Your physical health is like a fine performance vehicle. It needs a top-rated mechanic who knows the engines, sparks and tires. With regular fine-tuning, you can expect to run smoothly and sharp. But your soul is uniquely you. Everyone's got a distinct physiology once we peek into the DNA level. And thankfully so.

Let's start at the beginning. It takes courage to trust in life. Think about that. Courage. It takes courage to trust in what we don't see. From Thomas Edison envisioning electricity while seeing nothing, or any one of us experiencing a broken heart, it takes courage to choose to keep on trying, then trust just one more time.

COURAGE

Courage is the most important of all the virtues. Without it, you can't practice any of the other virtues consistently.

It takes courage to continue living even when life hits you hard with a curve ball. Something dies in each and every one of us if we allow our past to poison our heart. Within the word "compassion" lies "compass." Our true north is compassion and love. That is our key to life and what sustains us. It takes courage to have faith. It takes courage to believe life will get better when day-to-day evidence tells us otherwise.

The spiritual pillar contains all the others. At some point in life, most of us stop living out of imagination and start living in memory. That's the day we start dying. To be fully alive is to be fully present. It mandates leaving the past in the past. It requires living with faith.

KEEP LIVING

I believe we all have a spiritual tipping point. That tipping point is when the pain of staying the same becomes greater than the pain of change. You hit the kind of pain that forces you to believe in what you don't see with your eyes, but instead feel with your soul. You begin to live with wonderment, possibilities and the realism of something bigger than you. That's trust. So many lives are wasted on those who live in fear. Fear stymies people and they live the same day over and over again. Wisdom is letting go of fear because you have faith in trust.

The spiritual tipping point of your life allows you to get out of your comfort zone and trust. It allows you to have faith and believe in all the invisible aspects of life so you live rather than exist.

Humans were created to live and flourish. Growth is essential to life. If the tree stops growing, it dies. The same applies to humans -- in fact, everything in life.

Understanding this truth is a fundamental of spirituality. Without it, spirituality can actually become a problem for some. One spiritual problem is that we ask God to do for us without our making an effort to change. We repeat behaviors. It's as if we are driving down the road expecting to move in the forward direction to get to our destination, yet, looking in the rear view mirror the entire trip. Now how do you expect to go forward by doing that?

GOD HELPS THOSE...

We expect God to change our circumstances while we claim participation. Change is a two-sided coin. We must go out with the old behavior and in with the new. It is a team effort.

And to my belief, it is the reason to understand that the life force, God, is always with us. By allowing the spirit of God to flow through you and be the prime force, it's no longer just you alone -- it's a spiritual energy source.

This is where some people can become resistant. They believe I'm talking about religion. I am not. I am saying that religion is simply a map. Spirituality is the surrender.

When you allow yourself to turn toward God, you abandon the ego – a limiting ego full of fears and flaws -- and find a bigger truth. Letting go of the ego in so many ways sets us free. In today's world, we live in so much noise that we can't hear ourselves or anyone else. Each and every one of us has to spend time in the classroom of silence daily, whether in prayer, meditation, a walk in the woods, or free-style old fashioned silence. It is necessary. We must learn to be comfortable with silence. Even if for 30 seconds. If that's all you can do the first day, that's a good start. We can build it up, just as we grow from a five-minute walk to a 30-minute one. This is no different.

Building your spiritual strength is just like going from a bicep curl with five pounds to that of 25 pounds. You grow. To be spiritually fit, we must expand our time in silence. In a world that moves fast – and a culture that reeks of materialism - people fear silence. They are too often unfamiliar with their own thoughts. But this I know for sure: where you are is exactly where you need to be. It is your perfect starting point.

My greatest spiritual gift, other than my daughter, was hiking the Compostela de Santiago, a 543-mile hike through the Pyrenees Mountains starting in southern France and going from the east all the way to the west across the entire country of Spain. This trip was the most valuable time I have ever experienced. It was in that silence that I discovered my purpose, my meaning. Silence is necessary to develop spirituality, just as healthy eating enhances good health.

Advances in science have brought us a new term, Neurotheology. The book *How God Changes Your Brain*, (Ballentine Books, 2010), co-authored by Andrew Newberg and Mark Robert Walden, proves the advantages to your health by being thankful. The book points out that "Not only do prayer and spiritual practice reduce stress, but just 12-minutes of meditation per day may slow down the aging process." What a bonus on top of being more relaxed and happier.

Imagine, prayer creating that big a difference to your own physical and mental health. Just as the authors point out, we don't have to spend hours and hours. I believe that if you get into the habit of spending time in silence, prayer or meditation (or any other ways that bring you to quiet), you will have more clarity in life and build a fountain of strength. It never fails.

Some believe that the term God relates to religion only. It does not. Every culture taps into a different definition of this force. Even Hollywood. Think of "The Force" in George Lucas' blockbuster, "Star Wars." God is "The Force" behind all things. In other words, God is at heart the energy that created all things.

PUTTING TECHNOLOGY IN ITS PROPER PLACE

I have a theory that human beings have lost their spiritual groove as a result of the rapidly changing cultural and societal expectations that have resulted from technological advances. We have disconnected from the source within us all; we have lost the connection to the power greater than ourselves. To quote Austrian philosopher Rudolf Steiner, "Today we have seen what happens when natural science bypasses the human heart and translates knowledge into technology without grace, beauty or compassion." Words such as "grace," "beauty" and "compassion" are jam-packed with feeling and humanity. They are the words that make us human.

Our race to finish first has forced us to lose connection to these powerful concepts and what keeps us human. Even in my profession, the anti-aging movement -- which includes schools of professionals interested in cloning, striving to live a potential 120 years, and opting to change our exterior – there's much left to be desired. What about those qualities that make us human? Does the anti-aging movement inspire us to love our children more, bring more joy to the day, and realize our life's purpose?

Furthermore, what we include in our life is just as important as what we exclude. When we rid ourselves of toxins, what do we replace in that space? It's time to get serious about starting new habits – physical, intellectual, emotional and spiritual. The Four Pillars of Health.

The question I want you to ask yourself is *will I live longer* or *will it just feel like it's longer?* Only you can answer that. To quote American author and poet Maya Angelou, "I wish my words slide from your brain straight to your heart." It is time to create your map, your individual map that yours and yours alone. To reach our greatest potential, we must free our soul and allow it to evolve.

Without purpose we simply exist. With purpose, we experience the joy of living. So let's clean house. Start by forgiving yourself for past failures, when you know they were for good.

Without the test, there is no testimony. It's time to quit living as if the purpose of life is to arrive safely at death. Visualize playing cards with your buddies and when it's your turn, you say, "I'm all in!"

The spirituality pillar actually builds on the three others – the physical, emotional, and intellectual pillars. It's also the reason it's last. Like those other pillars, spirituality can be worked and improved.

Albert Einstein said, "There are two ways to live -- as if everything is a miracle or nothing is a miracle." Just as we chose a style of living, our spirituality is no different. Our world view -- or our perception of it – is full of choice. How do you envision it?

THE HARD QUESTION OF CONSCIOUSNESS

The topic of consciousness must be included in a discussion about spiritual health. We are perhaps more intimately driven by consciousness than we are of any other aspect of our health and lives for that matter. It makes up every ounce of our being. Yet we understand very little about it.

What is an idea? Where does it come from? What is a dream? How does it originate? Is it already existing within our innate intelligence? Just as the law of gravity exists, so too is the science of consciousness; it is God's reality and truth.

Is consciousness truth? Faith, I believe, is part of the law of consciousness. Illustrating this, here's one of my favorite quotes by Christian philosopher St. Augustine, born 354 A.D.: "Faith is to believe what you do not see; the reward of this faith is to see what you believe."

Faith is visionary. It is simply understood. You just "get it." Sometimes you are the only one, left to wonder why others don't. With that, sometimes in an effort to lead others to what you see, you may suffer.

All of life has a cause and effect. Each pillar of your health has a cause and effect:

- Eat poorly, get sick.
- Have toxic thoughts, get sick.
- Stay stagnant, never grow.

And all that is no different than "Garbage in-garbage out."

SOUL FOOD

Our souls need nutrition, as do our bodies. They hunger for nourishment. They long for expression and understanding.

Modern day spiritual leader and writer Marianne Williamson has said that consciousness has a cause and effect. What we think is seen as a result in our behavior. Such behavior is the effect of the cause and is seen as the end result in the behavior we display to the world.

ACTION STEPS

Now for the action steps (allowing you to raise your joy):

Awareness.

When you actually observe and raise awareness, you are living in the moment – just like the first grader on a field trip when everything is exciting.

Anyone who has met with the Dali Lama, Pope, or Mother Teresa, can tell you the feeling of being in their presence: as though they were the only person in the world. That is the now. Each of those spiritual leaders have been known to have that effect on people – and it is dramatic, life-altering and everlasting.

To work on raising your spirituality, here are seven action steps broken down individually. Normally, these would take split seconds to process, but I challenge you to consciously think through them one at a time.

Pause and feel yourself getting centered. This is where you work toward identifying yourself within who you are.

Step 1: Ask yourself: Am I thinking and acting as ego or spirit? Reframe as needed.

Step 2: Interpretation - What do I believe this to mean? Reframe as needed, again after being honest with myself.

Step 3: Belief - What is my world view? What do I believe about myself, others and the Universe?

Step 4: Orientation - Where am I coming from: my mood and/or attitude? In other words what is my starting point? Again, reframe after being honest with yourself.

Step 5: Intention -What is my purpose or motivation? Pause and answer honestly. Then reframe, if necessary.

Step 6: Action - What am I doing? What action has this caused me to take?

Lastly -

Step 7: Effect - What is the result of what I am doing?

In any spiritual exercise as with the above, it is worth slowing down the thinking process to become more aware if you are more ego- or spiritually-driven. Just as you learned to reframe your emotional health, you have complete control over reframing your spiritual health.

PURPOSE

We now get to purpose. Purpose is the lifeblood decision. The reason we are here. That which gives us life. Without purpose we simply exist.

Spirituality gives us purpose. It finds the way-the path for our purpose. It is through the journey, through the trial and error, through learning that we find that which gives us God bumps - those hairs that stand up on your arm also known as goose bumps that send a message to our soul that, *this is it.* It is the unrelenting force that makes us decide, change, and become ourselves through unity with our soul. Our alignment with consciousness. Dissecting it further, our legacy is the end result of our purpose. Our purpose created our intentions, which created our actions, with the end seen as the effect.

The spiritual pillar is perhaps the most mysterious, powerful and defining aspect of who we are. Just as we all have a different starting point for physical health, so too for the spiritual. And just like we now know we can up-regulate or down-regulate our physical health, so too our spiritual DNA. We can change. The world is surrounded by stories of those who have.

The only thing we leave this world with is our soul. Yet, as a culture we spend our lives working on the accumulation of the things that we can't take with us. The soul is the only part of our lives we take from the material world. It's time we consider this as a pivotal aspect of our health. To truly effect change in a world of frenetic energy, chaos and disorder, we must investigate and nurture our soul's purpose to really change humanity. It's not achieved through politics. Nor money. We can put Band-Aids on social problems all day every day and redirect attention and funds. As we have for decades. Yet the problems never change.

As Gandhi said, "Be the change you want to see in the world." It is grassroots. It is health. It is a realistic, attainable, goal-oriented project for our time.

We become physically sick when there is dis-order in our cells. We become spiritually sick when there is dis-order in our souls. The power lies within. The gift of life has been given to you out of love. And love is what binds us (just as misguided love is what divides us).

A great starting point? Love they neighbor. Begin with compassion if that's as far as you can get. Start daily with awareness and I guarantee a happier, more productive day while using your time more wisely. In doing so, you will see that health truly is more than simply the absence of disease. The only mystery you may uncover is why it took so long for you to uncover this. You'll discover that everything in life is a miracle. This simple yet profound look at your health will change your life.

You have been given the blue print in each area. Take the baby steps each and every day to a happier, healthier, more joy filled, and abundant life.

Today starts NOW!

Made in the USA
Middletown, DE
21 March 2020